PAUL BUNYAN

Troll Associates

PAUL BUNYAN

by Louis Sabin

Illustrated by Dick Smolinski

Troll Associates

Library of Congress Cataloging in Publication Data

Sabin, Louis.
   Paul Bunyan.

   Summary: Presents some of the extravagant feats of
the greatest logger of all time, Paul Bunyan.
      1. Bunyan, Paul (Legendary character)—Juvenile
literature.   [1. Bunyan, Paul (Legendary character)
2. Folklore—United States.   3. Tall tales]
I. Smolinski, Dick, ill.   II. Title.
PZ8.1.S213Pau   1985   398.2´2´0973   84-2747
ISBN 0-8167-0254-3 (lib. bdg.)
ISBN 0-8167-0255-1 (pbk.)

In every country throughout the world, there have been legends of bigger-than-life characters—characters who could do things no ordinary human being could do. In this long tradition, America has produced Pecos Bill, the fantastic cowboy, and Mike Fink, the incredible riverman. But no American folk hero can compare with Paul Bunyan, the giant logger, inventor, and doer of great deeds.

Nobody knows who told the first Paul Bunyan stories, or where or when. What is known is that they didn't appear in print until the early part of the twentieth century. Of course, the legends started long before that, as tall tales, which were dreamed up in lumber camps and mining camps. Wherever people had empty hours to fill, they turned to spinning tall tales of bravery, humor, and adventure.

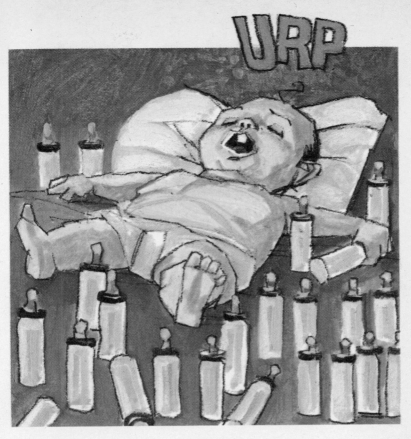

There are conflicting accounts of just where Paul was born. Some say it was in the state of Maine. Others say it was on Prince Edward Island, off the eastern shore of Canada. But all the storytellers agree that Paul weighed at least fifty pounds at birth. It took fourteen cows to supply enough milk to feed him at first. And every day he grew a couple of feet taller.

Right off, Paul was too big to sleep in a normal house. So his father built a huge cradle and set it in the Atlantic Ocean, near the coast. It seemed like a pretty good idea because the ocean waves could rock Baby Paul to sleep. Only it didn't work out the way it was planned.

Paul got bored just lying there, and he started bouncing up and down in his cradle. This caused a tidal wave that washed away three nearby villages. So Paul, who was getting too big for the cradle anyway, was brought back to land. And the wood from the cradle was used to rebuild all the villages.

The Bunyan family packed up and went to live in the woods. Paul's parents wanted to clear some land for farming. Paul, who was still a youngster, offered to help. In one day, he cleared more land than a hundred men could have cleared in a week. And before the sun had set, Paul had cut all the trees into logs. And that's how the logging industry was born!

Now, you may wonder just how big Paul Bunyan was. Well, when he was still a boy, he was so big that his shirt buttons were wagon wheels. In school he sat at four desks and wrote with a pencil he made out of a whole pine tree.

When he was fully grown, Paul Bunyan was so big that the tallest redwoods barely reached his belt buckle. His footprints made holes deep enough for small lakes to form. He had a thick black beard that was like a forest. And sometimes, in the winter, whole families of bears slept there until the spring thaw.

Paul was more than just big. He was so strong that he could pick up a team of horses and the wagon they were pulling, turn them around, and set them down on a narrow road. Paul was so fast, he could blow out a candle on one side of a room and be under his blankets on the other side before the light went out. His sense of humor was so sharp, he always knew when a joke was coming. So he started laughing when it was still miles away.

Paul was clever, too. He invented the two-
sided axe and the grindstone to sharpen it.
He also invented the crosscut saw. When he
wanted his logging crew to work after the
sun had set, he invented the aurora borealis,
or "northern lights." The northern lights
brightened up the sky and gave his loggers
the light they needed to work all night long.

There's no end to the wonderful things Paul did. He dug the channel for the St. Lawrence River, so that people would know if they were in Canada or the United States.

Why, even when he wasn't trying, Paul did great things. Once, when he was tired after a long day's work, he dragged his axe on the ground behind him. The result was a mile-deep groove we call the Grand Canyon.

But not even Paul Bunyan could do everything without some help—which is why it was lucky that he had his blue ox, Babe. Babe was born during the year of the Blue Snow. It was called that because the temperature was so low that even the snow turned blue with cold. And so did Babe as soon as he was born.

Babe was huge—just the right size for Paul. His eyes were so far apart that forty-two axe handles could fit between them. One day, a baby crow decided to fly from the tip of one of Babe's horns to the other. By the time it finished the trip, it had grown into an old crow.

Taking care of Babe was a big job. It took a whole iron mine to supply enough metal to make one set of shoes for the blue ox. His appetite was mighty big, too. He ate a ton and a half of hay every evening, with three wagonloads of turnips for dessert.

All that food made Babe so thirsty that he could never get enough to drink. Finally, Paul dug the Great Lakes—and that helped to quench Babe's thirst!

Feeding Paul and his logging crew was an even bigger job than feeding Babe. There were two hundred cooks in the kitchen, and the dining room had tables that were six miles long. Thousands of gallons of soup were made in an enormous kettle every day. The kettle was so big that Hot Biscuit Slim— the camp cook—had to use a rowboat to get from one side of the kettle to the other.

In Paul Bunyan's logging camp, Sourdough Sam was in charge of pancakes. He cooked them on a ten-acre griddle made by the camp blacksmith. To grease the griddle, four hundred assistant cooks skated over the hot metal surface with flat sides of bacon on their feet. Then the batter was poured onto the griddle from a giant hose.

Paul usually downed twelve or fourteen of those ten-acre pancakes all by himself. Paul Bunyan and his loggers ate a lot because they worked very hard. Paul and his seven axemen cleared all the forests in North Dakota in just one month. With every step they took, they chopped down one hundred sixty acres of timber.

Paul and his logging gang faced all kinds of problems as they worked their way across the country. One time they were cutting timber in a swamp, when they were attacked by a swarm of mosquitoes. Only these weren't everyday mosquitoes. They were more than a foot long and as mean as they were big. These bugs were said to sharpen their stingers on a grindstone till they were like razors.

Paul and his crew couldn't work while they were fighting off the mosquitoes. So Paul's chief bookkeeper, Johnny Inkslinger, came up with an idea. He sent away for the fiercest bees in the country.

But instead of chasing away the mosquitoes, the bees married them! Pretty soon, there were thousands of little "mosquitobees" flying around. They had stingers in front *and* back, so they got you both coming and going.

Then the camp blacksmith had an idea. He put some maple syrup under the pancake griddle. The mosquitobees dived down, trying to get the syrup, and ended up plunging their stingers right through the griddle.

Paul's crew was underneath the griddle. They quickly bent the ends of the stingers over, so the mosquitobees couldn't pull back

out. Those bugs got so angry that they flew off, taking the griddle with them.

But they didn't get very far. The weight of the huge griddle was too much for them, and it dragged them down until they tumbled into Moosehead Lake and sank to the bottom and drowned. That's why you never see any mosquitobees today.

After a while, Paul retired from the logging business. Some folks say he takes on a special job every now and then—like using a giant-sized slingshot to send missiles out into space.

Others say he doesn't do anything anymore. But you know he's around, because his cough sounds like thunder...and his footsteps are so heavy that they cause earthquakes. And just about everyone agrees that there will never be anyone as big or as strong or as mighty as the greatest logger who ever lived—Paul Bunyan.